EXTREME
DINOS

by
Suzanne Francis

with
Matthew T. Carrano, Ph.D.
Consultant

Scholastic Inc.

New York   Toronto   London   Auckland   Sydney
Mexico City   New Delhi   Hong Kong   Buenos Aires

ISBN 0-439-83873-8

Designers: Bob Budiansky and Lee Kaplan.

Cover illustration: *Troodon* © Todd Marshall.

Back cover illustration: (Dinosaur) © Falk Kienas/Shutterstock.com.

All Ty the *Tyrannosaurus rex* illustrations by Ed Shems.

All 3-D conversions by Pinsharp 3D Graphics.

Interior Photo and Illustration Credits:
Page 1: (Dinosaur) © Falk Kienas/Shutterstock.com.
Pages 4–5: *Dilophosaurus* © Julius Csotonyi; *Neuquensaurus* © Stephen Missal.
Pages 6–7: *Eotyrannus* © Todd Marshall.
Page 8: *Argentinosaurus* © John Bindon.
Page 9: *Microraptor* © Julius Csotonyi.
Page 10: *Troodon* © Todd Marshall.
Page 11: *Stegosaurus* © Jaime Chirinos.
Page 12: *Dromiceiomimus* © Julius Csotonyi.
Page 13: (*Pentaceratops* skeleton) © Kris Kripchak.
Page 14: *Pachycephalosaurus* © Julius Csotonyi; (pachycephalosaur skull) © Kris Kripchak.
Page 15: *Sauroposeidon* © H. Kyoht Luterman.
Page 16: (Hadrosaur jaw) © Kris Kripchak; (*T. rex* tooth) © Kris Kripchak.
Page 17: *Incisivosaurus* © Stephen Missal; *Pelecanimimus* © H. Kyoht Luterman.
Pages 18–19: *Edmontosaurus* © Todd Marshall; *Dromiceiomimus* © Julius Csotonyi.
Page 20: *Mononykus* © Pavel Riha; *Shuvuuia* © Julius Csotonyi.
Page 21: *Micropachycephalosaurus* © H. Kyoht Luterman.
Page 22: *Mei* © Julius Csotonyi.
Page 23: *Cryolophosaurus* © Joe Tucciarone; (Elvis Presley) © MGM/Photofest; *Gojirasaurus* © Stephen Missal; (Godzilla) © Toho/Photofest.
Page 24: *Apatosaurus* © H. Kyoht Luterman.
Page 25: *Megalosaurus* © H. Kyoht Luterman.
Pages 26–27: (*Diplodocus* spine) © Kris Kripchak; (*Diplodocus* skeleton) © Kris Kripchak; *Diplodocus* illustration © Todd Marshall.
Page 28: *Brachylophosaurus* © Stephen Missal; (Leonardo) © Judith River Dinosaur Institute, 2005.
Page 29: *Herrerasaurus* © Julius Csotonyi.
Page 30: (Karen Chin) © Louie Psihoyos/Corbis.
Page 31: *Amargasaurus* © Todd Marshall.
Page 32: *Coelophysis* © Karl Huber.

12 11 10 9 8 7 6 5 4 3 2   6 7 8 9 10 11/0

Printed in the U.S.A.

First Scholastic printing, May 2006

TABLE OF CONTENTS

Dilophosaurus
(die-LOAF-oh-SOR-uhss)

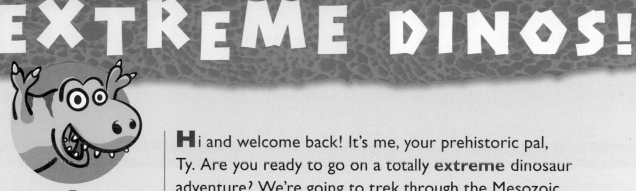

EXTREME DINOS!

Ty
Tyrannosaurus rex
(tie-RAN-oh-SOR-uhss
RECKS)

Hi and welcome back! It's me, your prehistoric pal, Ty. Are you ready to go on a totally **extreme** dinosaur adventure? We're going to trek through the Mesozoic and check out the most incredible dinosaurs. That's right! We'll meet the biggest, the fastest, the smartest, and many more! Did you know that:

◆ Some dinos had skulls that were like helmets?

◆ Scientists think one dino may have blown its nose up like a balloon?

◆ Other dinos were as tall as a four-story building?

And we'll answer all kinds of interesting questions like:

◆ Which dino was the smartest?

◆ Which dino has the coolest nickname?

◆ What was the longest dino fossil ever?

Remember to put on your **3-D glasses** when you see this icon for some extreme, in-your-face dino action!

Neuquensaurus
(NAY-oo-cane-SOR-uhss)

Are you ready to start our adventure? Come on! Follow the tracks and let's get moving!

5

Let's face it—dinos were a pretty weird group of animals. And scientists keep discovering new ones that are even bigger and stranger than the dinos we already know. But just because something's strange doesn't mean it isn't cool— like dinos!

Yup, it's true. We rocked!

In this book, we'll meet some of the strangest and most incredible dinosaurs that ever lived. We'll start with **Extreme Size, Smarts, and Speed** and take a look at the biggest, smallest, smartest, and fastest dinos the Mesozoic had to offer. Then we'll move on to **Extreme From Head to Tail** where we'll learn about unusual dinos with weird features—such as which dino had the goofiest grin, which had the strangest schnoz, and which was the biggest bonehead. We'll even meet two dinos who win the worst high-five award!

Next, check out **Extreme Names** and meet the dino with the longest name ever, a dino named after a movie monster, and a dino that's so nice they named it twice! Then we'll dig up the dirt on extreme fossils in the **Freaky Fossils** section. Find out which fossil is the longest ever found, which is the oldest, and even meet a dino mummy.

It's time to get going—we've got a lot of dinos to cover!

Eotyrannus
(EE-oh-tie-RAN-uhss)

GET EXTREME!

EXTREME
SIZE, SMARTS, AND SPEED

Large and In Charge

Dinos were some of the largest animals ever, so which dino was the biggest? Meet *Argentinosaurus* (are-jen-TEEN-oh-SOR-uhss), a plant-eating dino that lived during the Early Cretaceous 99 million years ago. *Argentinosaurus* was the biggest and heaviest dino ever and the largest land animal to walk the Earth!

How big is BIG? *Argentinosaurus* was about 45 feet (14 m) tall, 100 feet (30½ m) long, and weighed in at 80 tons. This dino was almost as long as a modern-day blue whale!

DINO DATA

When it was growing the fastest, *Argentinosaurus* probably gained about 100 pounds (45 kg) a day!

A herd of *Argentinosaurus*

Most Mini

Microraptor (MY-kroh-RAP-tore) wins the title of smallest dino—
claws down! This meat-eating dino lived during the Early Cretaceous,
about 130 million years ago. When *Microraptor* was discovered in 2001 in
northeastern China, scientists found that it was only
about 16 inches (41 cm) long—the size of a crow.

Microraptor also had a feathery coat and
long feathers on its legs and arms, which
is why it's sometimes called the "four-
winged" dinosaur. But scientists don't
think that *Microraptor* flapped its
wings and flew. This dino probably
used its wings to glide short
distances. Some scientists think
that *Microraptor* was **arboreal**
(are-BORE-ee-al), since it
had a long toe that could've
been used to hook onto tree
branches.

**Microraptor
and prey**

Dino Dictionary

Arboreal describes
animals that live
in trees.

9

Troodon

DINO DATA
A man named Ferdinand Hayden found the first *Troodon* fossil in 1855 in Montana. All he found was one tooth!

Head of the Class

Troodon (TROH-uh-don) lived 76 million years ago during the Late Cretaceous. Scientists consider *Troodon* the brainiest dino known today since it had a large brain for its body size (see **Dino IQ** on page 11 for more!). This smarty-saur was a meat-eating dino that was about 6 feet (2 m) long and weighed about 100 pounds (45 kg). Even though *Troodon* was much smaller than other meat-eaters like *Tyrannosaurus rex*, it was one of the deadliest dinos because of its sharp senses and big brain.

DINO IQ

Scientists can guess how smart a dino is by looking at how big its brain is compared to its body. Most of the info on dino brains comes from skull fossils. Scientists make **endocasts** (EN-doh-casts) to get an idea of what a dino's brain looked like. Small dinos usually had large brains compared to their body size, so they were clever for a dino—about as smart as an ostrich.

Dino Dictionary

An *endocast* is a mold of a brain made from the inside of a skull.

Mind Over Meatball

Large dinos probably weren't the brightest bunch in the Mesozoic. Their brains were small compared to their big ol' bodies. Big dinos like **stegosaurs** (STEG-oh-SORS), **sauropods** (SAW-roh-pods), and **ankylosaurs** (ang-KYE-loh-SORS) had brains about the size of meatballs! They probably weren't much smarter than your average iguana.

Stegosaurus (STEG-oh-SOR-uhss)

Meatballs? Where's the spaghetti?

DINO DATA

So dinos couldn't do crossword puzzles and crack codes. But they still could survive! As long as dinos had sharp senses, they had good chances of living in the Mesozoic.

Track Star

A group of dinos called **ornithomimids** (or-NITH-oh-MY-mids) were the speediest dinos back in the Age of Reptiles. Dinos in this group could kick up dust running up to 40 miles (64 km) an hour. That's faster than a racehorse! What made these dinos so fast? Ornithomimids had long legs and light bodies—everything that you need to be a speedy-saur.

Dromiceiomimus
(droh-MISS-ee-oh-MY-muhss)

FROM HEAD TO TAIL

So now that we've looked at the biggest, fastest, and smallest dinos, it's time to catch up with some dinos with some extraordinary bodies. Read on to explore these extreme dinos from head to tail!

Biggest Head

Pentaceratops (PEN-tah-SER-uh-tops) was a 28-foot (8½-m) dino from the Late Cretaceous. This dino's extreme feature was easy to spot—*Pentaceratops* had the largest head of any land animal. Its noggin measured almost 10 feet (3 m) from the tip of its nose to the back of its head—as long as a sports car!

   Pentaceratops was a member of a group of dinos called **ceratopsians** (SER-uh-TOP-see-ens). These dinosaurs had bony frills on the backs of their heads with a tough covering of bone or horn. This frill probably protected this dino from attacks by meat-eaters. It came in handy when *Pentaceratops* was trying to attract a mate, too.

Pentaceratops was definitely a-head of all the rest!

Pentaceratops skeleton

Pachycephalosaurus

Biggest Bonehead

Pachycephalosaurus (PACK-ee-SEFF-a-loh-SOR-uhss) lived during the Late Cretaceous, 75 million years ago. A plant-eating dino about 15 feet (4½ m) long, *Pachycephalosaurus* was named for its strange, dome-shaped head. Its name means "thick-headed lizard." Why "thick-headed"? Its skull had a 10-inch (25-cm) thick layer of bone— 20 times thicker than a human skull! This layer of bone probably protected this dino, making *Pachycephalosaurus* a real helmet head!

Talk about using your noggin!

HARD-**HEADED**

Some scientists used to think that a group of dinos called **pachycephalosaurs** (PACK-ee-SEFF-a-loh-SORS) used their thick skulls to bang heads when fighting over mates or living space. Now most scientists think that pachycephalosaurs' skulls and necks weren't built for head-butting. They probably used their heads to smash into the sides of other pachycephalosaurs or predators. A good whack might've helped an enemy get the message!

Pachycephalosaur skull

Check the Neck

Sauroposeidon (SOR-oh-poh-SYE-don) was an enormous dino that lived during the Early Cretaceous. This dino's extreme feature was its super-duper long neck. *Sauroposeidon* stretched 80 feet (24 m) from nose to tail and weighed about 50 tons. Its neck alone was 40 feet (12 m). That's half as long as its whole body! If *Sauroposeidon* were alive today, it could easily look into a fourth-floor window of a skyscraper.

How could this dino keep such a long neck up in the air? *Sauroposeidon*'s neck bones were very thin and light. This made lifting its massive neck easier. A long neck probably helped this dino reach branches and other green goodies in the Mesozoic.

Sauroposeidon

That's one heck of a neck!

Totally Toothy!

Back in the Mesozoic, the toothiest dinos around were a group of plant-eaters called **hadrosaurs** (HAD-roh-sors) that lived during the Late Cretaceous. These dinos, like *Edmontosaurus* (ed-MON-toe-SOR-uhss) on page 18, had toothless beaks like the ones on today's ducks, so they're also called "duck-billed" dinosaurs.

Toothless beaks? Where's the teeth?

Well, there weren't any teeth in the *front* of a hadrosaur's mouth. The back of the mouth was crammed with teeth—up to 960! These teeth were stacked in rows in the upper and lower jaws. While these dinos nearly had a thousand teeth in their mouths, only about 300 were used at one time to chew up prehistoric plants. Once the top row of teeth wore away, there was another set of teeth below to replace it.

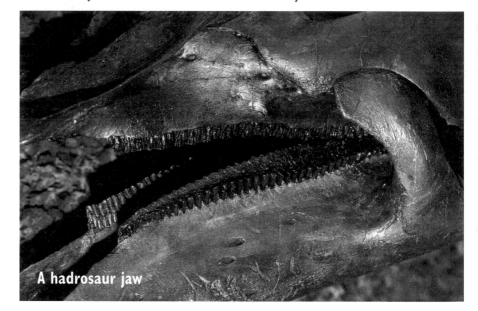

A hadrosaur jaw

T. rex tooth

LONG IN THE TOOTH

The dino that wins the award for the longest tooth is *Tyrannosaurus rex*. With a body up to 42 feet (13 m) long, *T. rex* was huge—and had gigantic teeth to match! *T. rex*'s teeth needed to be big and strong since this dino did some serious meat-eating. Its teeth needed to crush bone. The longest *T. rex* tooth ever found is about 7 inches (18 cm) in length—as long as an adult's hand!

Best Smile

Incisivosaurus (in-SICE-ih-voh-SOR-uhss) was definitely an odd-looking dino that wins the prize for most extreme smile. First of all, this turkey-sized dino from the Late Cretaceous (128 million years ago) only had a beak on its top jaw. There was no beak on its lower jaw. And if that wasn't weird enough, it had a pair of big teeth right in the front of its mouth. These unusual choppers earned *Incisivosaurus* the nickname "Rabbitosaurus."

While *Incisivosaurus* is a **theropod** (THAYR-oh-pod), a group of dinos that usually eat meat, this dino's unusual teeth make scientists think that *Incisivosaurus* was a plant-eater. Scientists guess that this dino chewed on seeds and hard plants and used **gastroliths** (GAS-troh-liths) to help digest big chunks of food.

Incisivosaurus

Dino Dictionary

Gastroliths are stones that animals swallow to help them grind up food.

TINY TEETH

Pelecanimimus (pell-ih-CAN-ih-MY-muhss) lived during the Early Cretaceous, about 121 million years ago. This weird-looking dino had a throat similar to a sea bird called a pelican, which is why its name means "pelican mimic." More than 200 teeth line the front of its upper and lower jaws—more teeth than any other meat-eating dino. But the teeth are tiny! Each one is about as big as the point of a pencil.

Pelecanimimus

Edmontosaurus

Strangest Schnoz

Edmontosaurus (ed-MON-toe-SOR-uhss) lived during the Late Cretaceous Period (65 million years ago) and was a hadrosaur or "duck-billed" dinosaur (turn to page 16 for more on hadrosaurs!). At 40 feet (12 m) long and weighing up to 4 tons, *Edmontosaurus*'s oddest feature was its nose. What was so strange about this dino's schnoz? *Edmontosaurus* might've had loose skin around its nose that it could blow up like a balloon. What a party trick! *Edmontosaurus*'s special schnoz could also make noise to warn other dinos of danger, find a mate, or even scare away enemies.

Jeepers Peepers

The dino with the largest eyes is **Dromiceiomimus** (droh-MISS-ee-oh-MY-muhss) which lived during the Late Cretaceous, about 75 million years ago. This dino was also a member of the ornithomimid group (see page 12 for more) and had large eyes and super-sharp eyesight. With very long legs, *Dromiceiomimus* was one of the fastest dinosaurs around. With its fast speed and good vision, *Dromiceiomimus* could have escaped larger meat-eaters. It probably ate small animals like insects and lizards, as well as plants.

Dromiceiomimus

DINO DATA

In 1909, a family of fossil hunters in Wyoming made a great discovery. They found two *Edmontosaurus* mummies. These fossils showed that these dinos had leathery skin that was covered with bumps in rows or patterns, like a football.

What big eyes you have!

Worst High-Five

The award for worst high-five is a tie between two dinos from the group **Alvarezsauridae** (AL-vah-rez-SOR-ih-day). Would you give them five?

How 'bout a high-two?

Shuvuuia (shoe-VOO-yuh) and *Mononykus* (MON-oh-NYE-kuss) were both turkey-sized dinos that walked on two legs and had long tails and necks. They were discovered in the Gobi Desert of Mongolia. *Shuvuuia* was named for the Mongolian word *shuvuu* which means "bird." *Mononykus* means "single claw." They both lived during the Late Cretaceous, about 85 million years ago. These dinos had feathers, but they couldn't fly.

Shuvuuia and *Mononykus* had extremely short, stubby arms with a single large claw at the end. It's a mystery what they used this strange claw for, but some scientists think they might have used this claw to poke around in dirt, tree bark, or insect nests to look for snacks like termites, bugs, and worms. Bug-licious!

Mononykus

Shuvuuia

DINO DATA

You might think that *Shuvuuia* and *Mononykus* look a lot like birds—and it's not just the feathers! When scientists discovered these two dinos, they saw that parts of their skeletons looked a lot like modern-day birds. *Shuvuuia* and *Mononykus* help support the idea that birds and dinos are directly related.

EXTREME NAMES

Wonder how dinos get their weird and wacky names? Scientists usually give a Latin or Greek name that describes what the dino looked like, or they name it after the place it was found. Sometimes scientists pick out some strange names for the dinos they discover. Check out these pages to meet a few dinos with some extreme names!

Tongue Twister

Try and say *Micropachycephalosaurus* (MIKE-roh-PACK-ee-SEFF-a-loh-SOR-uhss) three times fast. It's a Mesozoic mouthful! With 23 letters, this is the longest dino name on record—and there are some long ones! *Micropachycephalosaurus* lived 73 million years ago, during the Late Cretaceous, and was another bonehead dino like *Pachycephalosaurus* on page 14. While *Micropachycephalosaurus* had a gigantic name, it wasn't a very big dino. It was only about 2 feet (½ m) long, weighed around 30 pounds (14 kg), and is one of the smallest dinos known. Only very few of its bones were found, so scientists don't know much about this little dino with the giant name.

Micropachycephalosaurus

That's a long name for such a little dino!

Short and Sweet

Mei (MAY) wins the award for the dinosaur with the shortest (and sweetest!) name. This duck-sized dino was discovered in China in 2004. *Mei* had a large brain for its size, so scientists think that it was a smarty-saur. It also had long legs, suggesting that it was a fast runner. This dinosaur was a **troodontid** (TROH-uh-don-tid), one of the most bird-like groups of theropods. Many scientists think *Mei* is a link proving that birds are related to dinosaurs.

Mei

CATCHING ZZZZZs

Scientists found the *Mei* fossil in an interesting pose: it might have been taking a nap! Its head was tucked between its elbow and body and its tail was wrapped around it. This dino's full name, *Mei long*, means "soundly sleeping dragon." The fossil was preserved in layers of volcanic rock that were 130 million years old, so scientists guess that this dino was killed by poisonous gas from a volcanic eruption and buried in ash. It's very rare to find a dinosaur in a sleeping pose like *Mei*.

Funny Bones

Q: What do you call a dino that's fast asleep?

A: A dino-*snore*!

Your Name Rocks

Cryolophosaurus (cry-oh-LOAF-oh-SOR-uhss) lived during the Early Jurassic, 195 million years ago. This dinosaur was discovered in 1991 in Antarctica, making it the first meat-eater found on the icy continent.

Cryolophosaurus had a large head with a strange, bony crest that started just over its eyes and fanned out. Since the crest was very thin, scientists think that it was just for show—not for fighting. This strange crest inspired this dinosaur's ultra-hip nickname: "Elvisaurus." It reminded scientists of Elvis Presley, a rock-and-roll star in the 1950s. Can you see why? (Pssst! It's all in the hairdo!)

Cryolophosaurus

Elvis Presley

Gojirasaurus

Most Movie-Friendly

Gojirasaurus (go-JEER-uh-SOR-uhss) was a theropod from the Late Triassic, 210 million years ago. Paleontologist Ken Carpenter, who discovered this dino in 1997, is a big fan of a Japanese movie called *Godzilla* about a giant dino-monster. He named this new discovery after the famous movie monster using the original Japanese name "Gojira."

Gojirasaurus wasn't anywhere near as big as Godzilla—just over 18 feet (5½ m) long. No dino was as big as Godzilla. That monster chomped on train cars in downtown Tokyo like they were sticks of gum!

Godzilla

Double that Dino

Apatosaurus (uh-PAT-oh-SOR-uhss) was a dino that lived during the Late Jurassic, about 145 million years ago. This dino's name is interesting because, for a while, it had two! Yup, scientists once thought that there were two dinos, *Apatosaurus* and ***Brontosaurus*** (BRON-toe-SOR-uhss), when it was actually one dino all along. How did this happen? It all started in the late 1800s during the Bone Wars.

Apatosaurus

Dino Dictionary

The Bone Wars was a time when there was a rush to find and discover dinosaurs.

In 1877, paleontologist Othniel Charles Marsh and his team discovered a few dino bones. Marsh named this dinosaur *Apatosaurus*. A few years later, Marsh's crew found more bones and claimed it was a whole new dinosaur. He called it *Brontosaurus*. In 1903, a paleontologist named Elmer Riggs took a look at the bones that Marsh had found and figured something out: *Brontosaurus* and *Apatosaurus* were really the very same dino! Since *Apatosaurus* was the first name used, it's this dino's official name. But *Brontosaurus* stuck around for a really long time—you might still hear some people use it today!

FREAKY FOSSILS

Since we know dinos are long gone, the next best thing that scientists use to study them is fossils. And since we already know that dinos were really strange, sometimes the fossils that scientists dig up are strange, too! Read on to find out about some of the most extreme fossils that have ever been discovered.

First Dino Discovered

Back in the 1670s, before anyone had even heard of dinos, an English scientist named Robert Plot found a huge fossil of a thighbone. Plot had no idea what the bone was from. He thought it belonged to giant humans that once walked the earth!

 That's a really BIG idea!

Megalosaurus

Over the next 150 years, more huge bones kept turning up. Finally, another English scientist, William Buckland, took a look at them and decided that they were from a strange reptile. He named this reptile *Megalosaurus* (MEG-uh-loh-SOR-uhss), which is Greek for "great lizard."

DINO DATA

It wasn't until 1842 that scientist Richard Owen named this strange group of reptiles "dinosaurs."

The Longest Fossil

Diplodocus (dih-PLOD-oh-kuhss), a plant-eating dino that lived during the Late Jurassic 145 million years ago, is the longest dinosaur ever dug up. It was 90 feet (27 m) long! *Diplodocus* was named "double-beamed lizard" because of the way the bones of its spine fit together. A member of the sauropod family, *Diplodocus*'s neck and tail made up more than half its length. Its peg-like teeth at the front of its mouth were probably used to strip leaves off of branches. Like other plant-eaters, it swallowed stones to help it grind up all the leaves and branches it munched on. Its front legs were shorter than its back legs, and it had elephant-like, five-toed feet. One toe on each hand had a thumb claw—but scientists haven't figured out what this was for yet. A fossilized *Diplodocus* skin **impression** (im-PRESH-shun) reveals that it had a row of skin spines running down its back.

Dino Dictionary

An *impression* is the mark that's made when something (like dino skin) is pressed into a soft surface, like sand or mud.

Part of a *Diplodocus* backbone

Diplodocus

Diplodocus skeleton

Funny Bones

Q: Why do fossils sleep all day long?

A: Because they're lazy bones!

Best Mummy

Brachylophosaurus (BRACK-ee-LOAF-oh-SOR-uhss) lived during the Late Cretaceous, 78 million years ago. A **mummy** (MUM-mee) of a *Brachylophosaurus*, named "Leonardo," was discovered in Montana in 2000. Leonardo was about four years old when he died and is amazingly preserved. Scientists guess that this young *Brachylophosaurus* became trapped on a sandbar and dried out before he was covered with more sand. Over time, Leonardo fossilized so that 90% of his bones were covered in soft tissue like skin, muscles, nails, and a beak. You can even see leftovers of his last meal!

Brachylophosaurus

Brachylophosaurus was a duck-billed dinosaur. It was 23 feet (7 m) long and weighed 1½ tons. It had a tall head and its nose was short and curved down to its beak. Like the other hadrosaurs, it had hundreds of teeth (see page 16). It had a low, solid crest with a bump behind and between its eyes, which might have been used to attract mates.

Dino Dictionary

A *mummy* is any animal's body that has been dried out and preserved so it lasts a very long time. Ancient Egyptians made mummies out of people and animals on purpose, but sometimes a mummy forms naturally, like Leonardo.

Leonardo the dino mummy

Oldest Dino

Herrerasaurus (huh-RARE-uh-SOR-uhss) is the oldest known dinosaur. It lived during the Late Triassic, 225 million years ago. At 400 pounds (181 kg) and 17 feet (5 m) long, *Herrerasaurus* must have been an excellent hunter. It was fast, and had hands to grab and rip prey. Its double-hinged jaws and sharp teeth made it easy for *Herrerasaurus* to swallow huge chunks of meat.

225 million years? Those are some old bones!

Herrerasaurus and prey

DINO DATA

When *Herrerasaurus* was alive in the Triassic, dinosaurs didn't rule. *Herrerasaurus* and its early dinosaur cousins were rare. There were plenty of mammal-like reptiles around, but few dinosaurs. Those reptiles were no match for the dinosaurs though! Over the next 10 million years, dinos would replace most of the other large land animals.

Dr. Chin examining some possible coprolites.

Meet Karen Chin, a paleontologist at the University of Colorado. What's so extreme about what Dr. Chin studies? She's the world's leading expert on fossilized dino poop, called **coprolites** (KOP-proh-lites). What can you learn from dino dung? Read on to find out!

Q How did you get interested in coprolites?

A I used to work for the famous dinosaur paleontologist, Jack Horner, and he showed me some coprolites that he'd collected. Since I knew that scientists learn a lot about living animals by looking at their dung, I became interested in what we might learn about dinosaurs by studying coprolites.

Q Why is it important to study coprolites?

A Body fossils, like bones and shells, can tell us what an animal looked like, but can't tell us how it behaved or how it affected other living things when it was alive. Coprolites give us clues that can tell us what an animal ate, what plants and animals it lived with, and can even preserve tissues that are hard to fossilize, like bits of muscle.

Q What's the hardest thing about studying dino dung?

A It's hard to tell if something is really a coprolite—it could just be a rock! You have to study it very carefully. It's also very hard to find out which animal made a coprolite. If a coprolite is big, it's probably a good guess that it came from a dinosaur. But just because an animal is big doesn't mean it produces large droppings.

Q What other coprolite projects are you working on?

A I'm studying a group of Cretaceous coprolites from sea animals that lived above the Arctic Circle [near the North Pole]. This is pretty exciting because these fossils will tell us what marine environments looked like some 73 million years ago when the Arctic wasn't so cold.